THE USBORNE BOOK OF
EASY
VIOLIN
TUNES

Susan Mayes

Designed by Joanne Pedley

Illustrated by Adrienne Kern
(Additional illustrations by Peter Dennis)
Photography by Howard Allman

Music consultant: Rachel Sokolowski
Original music and arrangements by Caroline Hooper
Edited by Emma Danes

Series editor: Anthony Marks

About your violin

This book has lots of tunes for you to play on your violin, as well as tips to help you to improve your playing. If you read these two pages before you start, you will find out about the different parts of your violin, and some hints about how to take care of it.

The different parts

This picture shows what the parts of the violin and bow are called, and what some of them are for.

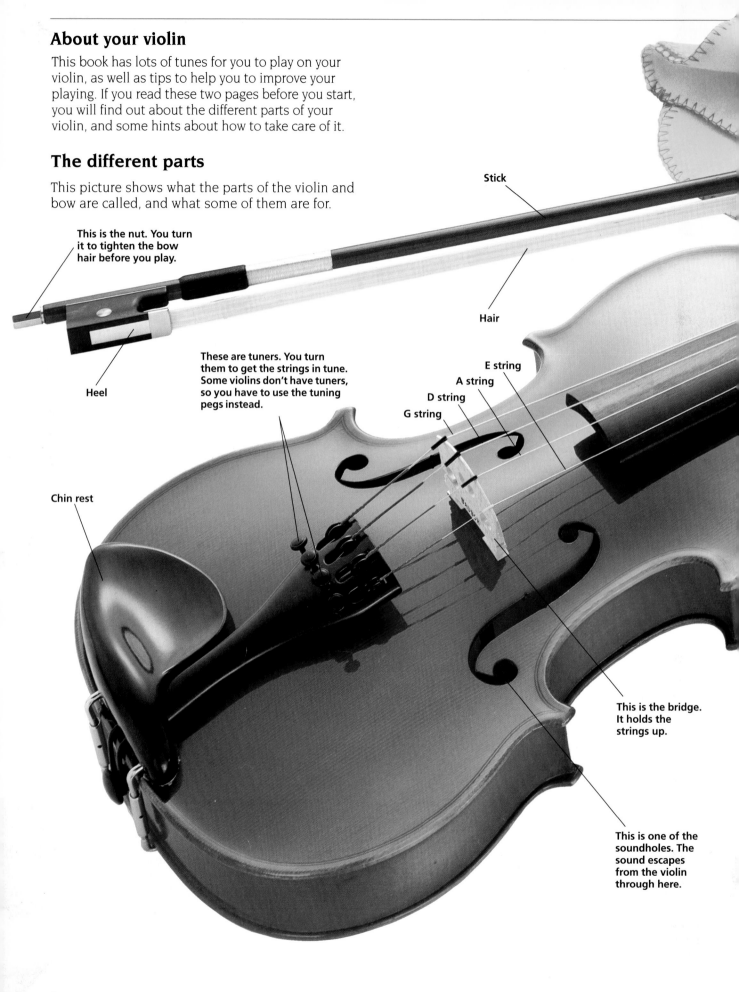

This is the nut. You turn it to tighten the bow hair before you play.

Heel

Stick

Hair

These are tuners. You turn them to get the strings in tune. Some violins don't have tuners, so you have to use the tuning pegs instead.

E string

A string

D string

G string

Chin rest

This is the bridge. It holds the strings up.

This is one of the soundholes. The sound escapes from the violin through here.

Point

Scroll

These are tuning pegs.
You can use them to
tune the strings, as
well as using the
tuners.

Fingerboard

Other things you need

You need two "extras" to go with
your violin. You need rosin, or
resin, to stop the bow from sliding
around on the strings. You also
need a shoulder pad or a shoulder
rest, to help you hold your violin
comfortably.

A sponge attached to
the violin with a rubber
band makes a good
shoulder pad.

Or you can buy a
shoulder rest, like
the one below, from
a music shop.

Rosin helps the bow
to grip the strings.
Rub some onto the
hair each time you
play. (It only works
when the shiny
surface has been
worn away.)

Looking after your violin

Here are some tips on keeping
your violin clean and in good
working order. There may seem
to be lots to remember, but if
you do these things they will help
your violin look and sound good.

Polish the wood to keep it clean and
shiny. You can buy cleaner specially
for this job from music shops. You can
clean the strings with rubbing alcohol from a
pharmacy, but never get any on the wood of the
violin because it will damage the varnish.

Try not to touch the bow
hair with your fingers. This
will make it greasy and
the bow may slip
on the strings.

Loosen the bow hair
when you finish
playing. To do this,
partly unscrew the
nut at the
bottom.

If one of
the hairs on your
bow breaks, cut the
pieces off carefully
at each end. Never
pull them out.

When
you put
your violin in
its case, wrap it in
a clean duster or cloth,
to protect it.

Tuning your violin

In order to sound right, the strings on your violin must play the correct notes. This is called being "in tune". When you are not playing your violin, it can go out of tune for many reasons. It may be too hot or cold, or a slight knock might alter the tuning. So each time you play, you have to begin by checking that each string is in tune.

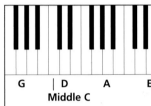

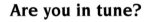

Tuning fork

Pitch pipes

The easiest way to tune up is to check your strings against a set of pitch pipes. There is a pipe for each one. Pitch pipes may not always be exactly in tune, but they will help to start with.

Once you are familiar with how the strings should sound, a tuning fork is a more reliable way to tune the first string. But you have to tune all the other strings "by ear", imagining how they should sound. This takes a little practice.

You could tune up by checking your strings against the notes shown on the right, played on a piano. You should always do this if you are going to play with a piano accompanying you.

Hit the tuning fork gently on your knee, then place it on a hard surface to hear the sound it makes.

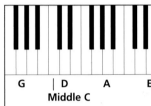

G | D | A | E
Middle C

This keyboard shows you the notes you will need for checking your strings. Begin with the A above middle C.

Are you in tune?

You always tune the A string first. This makes it easier to hear whether or not the other strings are in tune. Get the sound of the note A from your tuning fork, pitch pipe or piano. Now pluck the A string on your violin with your right thumb. Does it sound higher or lower than the tuning note?

If it sounds lower ("flat"), turn the tuner to the right. This will make the string sound higher. Go very slowly, checking the string against the tuning note, until the two sound the same. If it sounds higher ("sharp"), turn the tuner to the left. This makes the string sound lower.

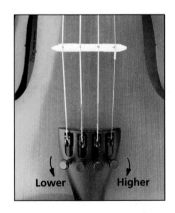

Lower   Higher

Once your A string is in tune, check the other strings. Most people tune the D string, then the G, then the E. This is the best way of hearing the strings properly.

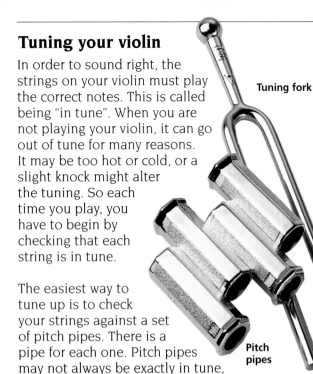

It is best to sit down while you tune your violin, so that you can hold it firmly.

Tuning tip

If your note is very out of tune, use the tuning peg instead of the tuner. Turn the peg away from you to make your note higher, and toward you to make it lower.

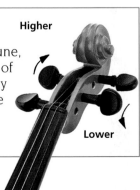

Higher

Lower

4

Holding the violin and the bow

If you hold the violin and bow properly when you play, you will feel comfortable and relaxed. This picture shows you the things to check when you stand or sit to play. You could try looking in a mirror to see if you are doing everything correctly.

Your shoulders should be relaxed.

Hold the violin between your jaw and your left shoulder, with only a little help from your left hand.

Your bowing arm should look like this. Make sure your elbow and wrist are relaxed, but not floppy.

Your left hand should look like this. It should feel relaxed and not grip the violin too hard. Your fingertips should be curved over the strings.

Your little finger should sit on the stick and your thumb should be curved underneath.

Try to keep your back fairly straight, but not too stiff.

Whether you stand or sit, your feet should be flat on the floor, a little way apart, to help you balance.

Holding up

Make sure you hold your violin firmly between your jaw and left shoulder. You should not need your left arm to hold it up. To see if you are holding it properly, try moving your left arm around. When you do this for the first time, do it over a soft surface.

Try touching your right shoulder or your nose with your left hand.

Lining up

Your left elbow should be tucked under the violin, not sticking out at the side. It should be under the strings, in an imaginary line down to the ground.

Your bow should be in line with the bridge like this. Try to keep it in line all the time when you are playing.

New notes

Play the tunes on these pages on the D string, using the notes D, E, F sharp and G, shown here. In this book, when you need to learn new notes, a box like this one shows you how they are written. A number above the note tells you which finger to use. "0" means "open string" (don't use any fingers).

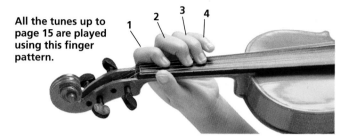

D E F# G

This sign is called a sharp. ♯

Positioning your fingers

The picture on the right shows you how to position your fingers to play the notes above. Your second and third fingers should be touching each other, but your first and second fingers should not. You could check that you are playing the notes in tune by listening to them played on a keyboard.

All the tunes up to page 15 are played using this finger pattern.

Bowing signs

This is the sign for a down bow. Pull the bow from the heel to the point.

This is the sign for an up bow. Push the bow from the point to the heel.

Violin music has bowing signs in it, to tell you whether to play an up bow or a down bow. Always check at the beginning of a tune, to see which bowing sign it starts with. Then continue by playing each note with a new bow-stroke, unless the signs tell you to do something different.

Note lengths

Note lengths are counted in beats. You can see the most common note lengths below. They also appear in all the tunes on these pages. Always try to count the beats evenly as you play and make sure each note lasts for the correct number of beats.

Quarter note = 1 beat

Half note = 2 beats

Whole note = 4 beats

Time signatures

Music is divided into sections called measures. The two numbers at the start are called a time signature. The top one tells you how many beats to count in a measure. The bottom number tells you what kind of beats they are ("4" means they are quarter notes).

This means there are 4 quarter note beats in a measure.

This means there are 3 quarter note beats in a measure.

Humming tune

Play this tune with your fingers in the position shown above. There are numbers at first, to remind you which fingers to use. Start with a down bow.

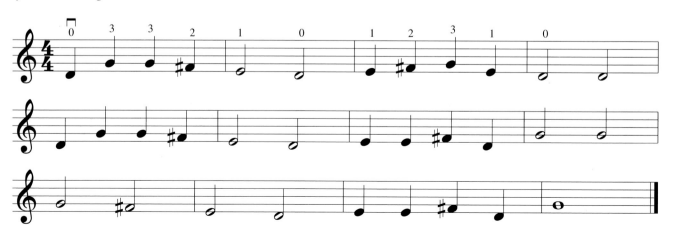

March tune

A sharp sign in front of a note tells you to play
that note sharp all the way through the measure.
Play F sharp all the way through this piece.

Rigaudon

This tune is by an English composer called Henry
Purcell (1659-1695). A rigaudon is a lively dance.

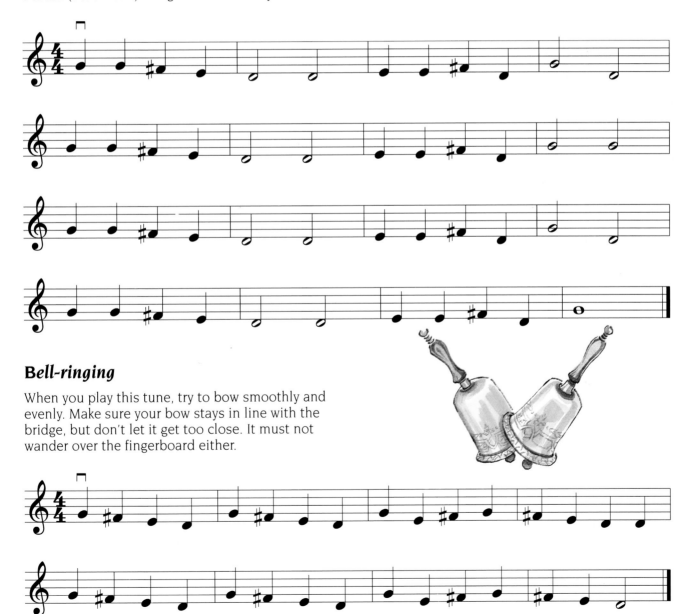

Bell-ringing

When you play this tune, try to bow smoothly and
evenly. Make sure your bow stays in line with the
bridge, but don't let it get too close. It must not
wander over the fingerboard either.

New notes

Here are the new notes that you will use on these pages. The tunes are mostly played on the A string, although you sometimes have to play the open E, too. For B, C sharp and D, use the same finger pattern that you learned on page 6, but move your fingers across to the A string.

Riding on a donkey

This old song uses all the notes shown above. The tune jumps up to open E near the end, so don't forget to move your bow over to the new string.

Eighth notes

Eighth note

Pair of eighth notes

Four eighth notes

An eighth note is half a quarter note beat long, so there are two eighth notes to every quarter note. Eighth notes can be written on their own or joined together in groups. Remember to make all the eighth notes the same length, and try not to rush them.

Two-string waltz

A waltz is a dance with three quarter note beats in a measure. Waltzes were very popular in the 19th century. Play this tune in the middle part of the bow. Try to bow firmly, and play the eighth notes evenly. Look for the open E notes.

Dotted notes

Dotted quarter note

The tunes on this page have dotted notes in them. A dot after a note increases its length by half as much again. A dotted quarter note is one and a half beats long. It is usually followed by an eighth note to make up the second beat. Clap the rhythm on the right by counting "one, two" on the dotted quarter note, then a quick "and" on the eighth note.

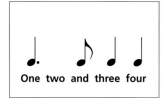

One two and three four

The old brown cow

Watch for the dotted quarter notes in this tune. Be careful not to rush them. If you find the rhythm tricky, try clapping it a few times. This will help you get to know it.

The conquering hero

This tune is by the German composer George Frideric Handel (1685-1759). It is from an oratorio, a type of piece written for a choir and orchestra on a religious subject. You can see one being performed on the right.

Using your bowing arm

Remember to hold your bow gently and to relax your bowing arm. Your hand and wrist should also be flexible as you play. They should make a mountain shape when the bow is at the heel and a valley shape when the bow is at the point. Doing this properly will help you to play smoothly and improve the sound you make.

Mountain shape

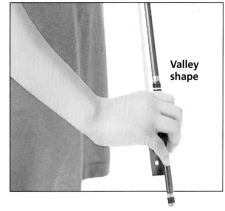

Valley shape

Over the hills and far away

This is a very old English folk song. There are lots of eighth notes in this tune. Count the quarter note beats steadily, and make sure you fit two eighth notes into each one. Be careful to change your fingers and bow at exactly the same time. It might help if you try this slowly at first.

Dotted half notes

2 + 1 = 3

A dot after a half note increases its length by half, making it a quarter note beat longer. So a dotted half note is three beats long altogether.

Rests

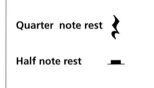

Quarter note rest

Half note rest

Silences in music are called rests. You count them just like notes. A quarter note rest lasts for one beat. A half note rest lasts for two beats.

Lightly row

This tune is another folk song. Play using plenty of bow, especially on the long notes. Try to use a whole bow when you play the half notes and the dotted half note. Remember to keep your bowing wrist flexible to help you change notes smoothly. There is a half note rest in the middle of the tune, so stop the bow on the string for two beats.

Tied notes

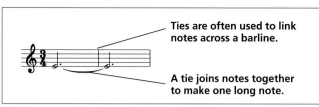

Ties are often used to link notes across a barline.

A tie joins notes together to make one long note.

Notes on the same line or space can be linked together to make one long note, using a curved line called a tie. When you see two tied notes, play them together in one long bow. As you play, count the same number of beats as the two notes added together.

Morning has broken

This tune was originally a folk song. It later became a hymn tune. When you play the long tied notes, don't move your right arm too quickly or you will run out of bow.

Key signatures

This key signature reminds you to play F sharp and C sharp all the way through the piece.

In the next piece, there are sharp signs before the 4/4 sign. They are called the key signature. The key signature tells you which notes to play sharp throughout the tune. You have to concentrate, so that you remember to play the correct notes.

Jumping beans

Remember to play F sharp and C sharp all the way through this tune. Keep your fingers in the pattern shown on page 6.

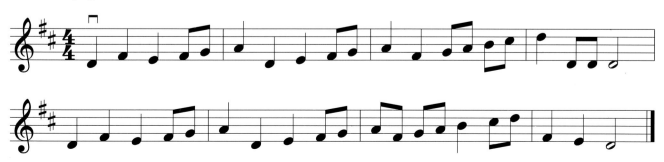

11

New notes

In the tunes on these pages, you have to play on the G string. The new notes you will use are G, A, B and C. You will need to raise your bowing arm a little bit to play them, but don't let your elbow get higher than your wrist. Use the same finger pattern that you learned on page 6.

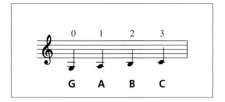

Slurred notes

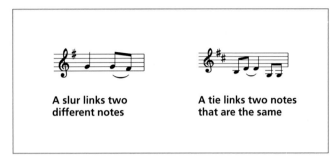

A slur links two different notes

A tie links two notes that are the same

Sometimes, you have to play two or more different notes together in one bow. These are called slurred notes. The sign that links slurred notes is like the one that links tied notes. You can tell the difference between a slur and a tie, because a slur links two different notes and a tie links two notes that are the same. To play slurred notes, keep the bow going in the same direction. Count carefully and change the left-hand fingering to play the next note.

Russian folk song

This tune is by the German composer, Ludwig van Beethoven (1770-1827), shown here. It is in 2/4 time, which means there are two quarter note beats in a measure. Look for all the slurred notes. The sign *f* means "play loudly". Find out more below.

Playing loudly

Signs in music that tell you how loudly to play are called dynamics. The sign *f* stands for *forte*, the Italian word for "loudly". Play loudly by bowing close to the bridge, but not too close or you will make a squeaking sound. Press a little harder as you play and use lots of bow. If you begin to make a creaky sound, then you are pressing too hard.

Stepping stones

The sign *mf* at the beginning of this tune stands for *mezzo forte*, which means "fairly loudly".

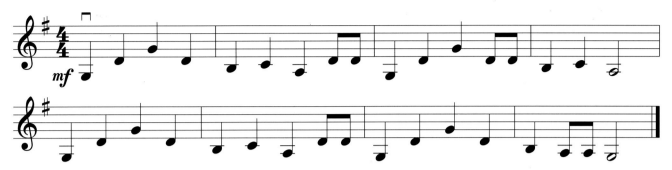

Up-beats

Some tunes begin part way through a measure, on a beat called an up-beat. A tune with an up-beat has an incomplete last measure, too. Together, the first and last measures make one full measure.

Count a silent "one, two", then play on "three".

Lullaby

This tune is by the German composer, Johannes Brahms (1833-1897). The sign *p* at the beginning tells you to play quietly. Find out more below.

Playing quietly

The sign *p* stands for *piano*, the Italian word for "quietly". To play quietly, don't press as hard, and play a little nearer the fingerboard, too. Tilt the bow away from you slightly, so you only play with a few of the hairs. Playing quietly takes practice to get good bow control, as the bow can slip around more easily when it is in this position.

New notes

In the tunes on these pages, you have to play on the E string. The new notes you will use are F sharp, G sharp and A. Use the same finger pattern that you used on page 6. In the next tune, the measure at the end of the first line will help you to practice playing these notes.

Cancan

This tune is by the composer Jacques Offenbach (1819-1880). The cancan is a dance with lots of high kicks. The word *allegro* at the beginning means "quickly". If you cannot play the tune quickly to begin with, practice it slowly, then speed up once you feel confident. Look for the quick string change in the last measure.

Pizzicato playing

Use the fleshy pad of your fingertip, not your fingernail.

Pull and release the string gently. Try not to tug at it.

Pizz. written in the music is short for the Italian word *pizzicato*. It tells you to pluck the string instead of playing it with the bow. You can put your bow down to do this. Then place your right thumb at the corner of the fingerboard. Place your first fingertip on the string, over the fingerboard. Pluck the string by pulling it gently and releasing it. The pictures on the left show you how to do this.

The gazelles

When you play this pizzicato piece, count the beats carefully to make sure you don't rush the long notes. The word *andante* at the beginning means "at a walking pace".

Eighth note rests

An eighth note rest lasts for half a quarter note beat. It is often followed by an eighth note, to make up one whole beat. This happens in the next tune. Practice the rhythm on the right. Stop playing on the word "four", then play the eighth note on the word "and".

Eighth note rest

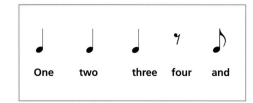

One   two   three   four   and

Hither, dear husband

This tune is from *The Beggars' Opera*, a musical show written by John Gay (1685-1732). You can see a scene from the show on the right. *Moderato* at the beginning means "at a moderate speed", a little faster than *andante*. Start with an up bow.

Slumber song

The words *con sordino* in this tune tell you to use a mute (a device that you place on your violin to make it quieter). You can buy a mute from a music shop. It fits onto the bridge, as shown in the picture on the right. (Always fit your mute carefully, and do not push it on too hard.) In this tune, keep your bowing arm relaxed and play with long bows.

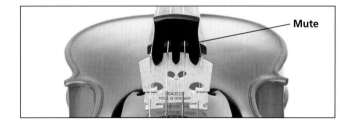

Mute

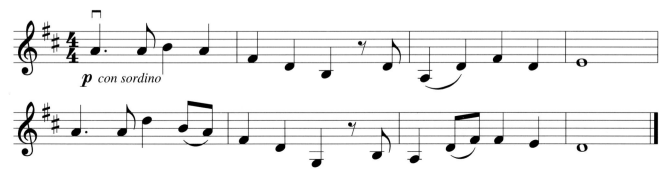

New notes

The new notes on these pages fit in the same spaces as the sharp notes you learned earlier in this book, but they do not have sharp signs in front. They are called naturals. They sound lower than the sharp notes and you play them with a different finger pattern. Find out more below.

A new finger pattern

On these pages, you have to play the F, C and G shown above. Your second finger should touch your first. Don't put it close to your third finger, as you do when you play F sharp, C sharp and G sharp.

Put your second finger close to your first finger, like this.

Song of the ass

This 12th-century song has F and C in it. Remember that these notes don't have sharp signs, and there are no sharps in the key signature. So play them using the new finger pattern above. The notes are marked with a "2" in the music, to remind you.

Castanet song

Georges Bizet (1838-1875), a French composer, wrote this tune. Castanets are wooden discs that make clicking sounds. You have to repeat this tune. Find out more on the right.

Repeating music

A repeat sign with dots on the left tells you to play the last section of music again. Go back to the start, or to the last repeat sign with dots on the right, if there is one.

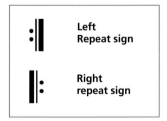

𝄆	Left Repeat sign
𝄇	Right repeat sign

Getting louder and quieter

Louder	Quieter

These signs are called crescendo and diminuendo. The sign that gets larger on the right is a crescendo. It tells you to get gradually louder. The sign that gets smaller on the right is a diminuendo. It tells you to get gradually quieter. To change the loudness of your playing, remember to change the way you use your bow. Look back at pages 12 and 13 to remind yourself.

What shall we do with the drunken sailor?

This is a type of tune originally sung by sailors, called a sea chantey. Get loud then quieter again at the end. Remember to play the new C and G notes. Look for the high F sharp in the second line.

Drink to me only

This tune is in 6/8 time. This means there are six eighth note beats in a measure, arranged in two groups of three. You can count eighth notes, or two dotted quarter notes in each measure. Look for the slurred eighth notes, and remember that you have to play C naturals all the way through the piece. There is a G natural in line three.

Crescendo and diminuendo

Cresc. is short for the Italian word *crescendo*. It means "get gradually louder". *Dim.* is short for the Italian word *diminuendo*. It means "get gradually quieter". These words mean the same as the signs at the top of the page. When you see them in the music, get gradually louder or quieter until you reach the next sign that tells you how loud to play.

New notes

You play the new notes on these pages on the A string and the E string. You have to use your first finger. You can find out more about the new finger pattern below. Whenever you learn a new note, compare it with the open string, to get used to how it sounds.

This sign is called a flat.

A new finger pattern

To play the new notes above, first place your fingers in the pattern shown on page 16. Then pull your first finger back as far as you can toward the scroll, leaving a gap between your first and second fingers.

There is now a space between your first and second fingers, as well as between your second and third.

Theme from symphony no.6

This tune is by the Russian composer Pyotr Il'yich Tchaikovsky (1840-1893). It is from one of his large pieces for orchestra, called a symphony. Use the new finger pattern for the note F, on the E string. There is some new bowing, too. Find out more below.

New bowing

In lines two and three of the tune above, there are two down bows, one after the other. After the first down bow, take the bow off the string. Move it up quickly and place it on the new string, near the heel, ready to play a completely new down bow. The pictures on the right show you how.

When you see two up bows, one after the other, don't take your bow off the string for the second up bow. Just stop the bow after the first note, then continue bowing in the same direction after the rest.

End of first down bow

Beginning of second down bow

Practice piece

Play this short piece to help you practice the new first finger notes shown on page 18.

The sign **ff** at the beginning stands for *fortissimo*, which means "very loudly".

The Londonderry Air

An Irish violinist is said to have made this tune famous. Remember to play the new B flat and F.

Nocturne

This piece by Felix Mendelssohn (1809-1847) was inspired by William Shakespeare's play A *Midsummer Night's Dream*. Remember to play B flat throughout.

A scene from
A Midsummer Night's Dream

Dotted quarter note rests

Dotted quarter note rest

A dot after a rest increases its length by half. A dotted quarter note rest is one and a half quarter note beats long. As the tune below is in 6/8 time, either count eighth note beats and allow three for each rest, or count in dotted quarter note beats and allow one for each rest.

Eighth notes
One two three   four five six
One   two
Dotted quarter notes

Sumer is icumen in

This song was written in the 14th century. A manuscript of the opening measures is shown on the right. Use the finger pattern shown on page 18 when you play on the A string and the E string. Look for all the new down bows.

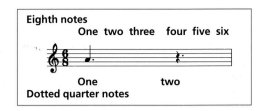

Playing a round

A round is a tune which can be played by two or more people, starting a few measures after each other. You can play the tune above as a round, with a friend. They could play the violin too, or another instrument, such as a recorder or keyboard.

One of you starts playing from the beginning. When the first player reaches the third measure, the second player starts from the beginning. You must both count the beats very carefully. A third player could start when the second player reaches measure three.

20

New notes

The new notes you will need on this page are shown on the right. You have to use a different finger pattern for each one. To play the E flat, pull your first finger back toward the scroll, as you did on page 18. Play the low B flat on the G string, with your fingers in the pattern you learned on page 16.

E♭ B♭

The Hunt Quartet

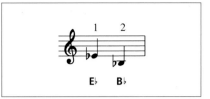

This tune is by Wolfgang Amadeus Mozart (1756-1791), shown here. A quartet is a piece for four players, each playing a separate line of music. Pull your first finger back when you play on the D string, but keep it in the normal position on the G string.

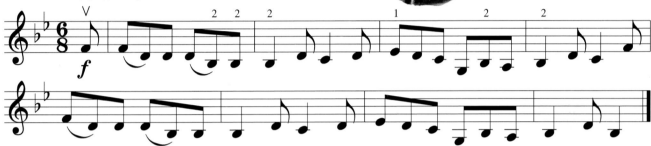

Accents

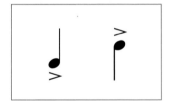

An accent sign is written above or below a note to show that it should be emphasized. When you see an accented note, play it a little louder than the others. To play an accent, press a little harder at the beginning of the note, then release the pressure quickly as you move the bow.

The Israeli national flag

Hatikvah

This is an old Jewish melody. It is used as the Israeli national anthem. *Hatikvah* means "hope". Repeat the first section and don't play the accents too heavily.

21

Sixteenth notes

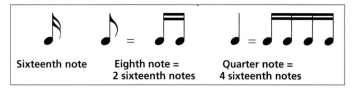

| Sixteenth note | Eighth note = 2 sixteenth notes | Quarter note = 4 sixteenth notes |

A sixteenth note lasts for half an eighth note. Sixteenth notes are mostly written in groups and joined together by two lines called bars. Two sixteenth notes last for an eighth note and four sixteenth notes last for a quarter note.

Strawberry fair

This English folk song has lots of sixteenth notes in it. Clap the rhythm all the way through before you play the tune. Don't play too fast, or it will be difficult to fit the sixteenth notes in.

Accidentals

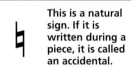

This is a natural sign. If it is written during a piece, it is called an accidental.

An accidental is a sharp, flat or natural sign that is written during a tune, but is not in the key signature. Accidentals go before the note they change. They affect all the notes in the same line or space, but only for the length of that measure.

Le petit rien

This tune is by a French composer called François Couperin (1668-1733), who was the organist at the church shown here. The sign **mp** stands for *mezzo piano*, which means "fairly quietly". The key signature has F sharp and C sharp, but look for the place where you play a C natural accidental.

Aria Allemagna

This tune was written by Alessandro Poglietti (died 1683). He composed it for an instrument called a harpsichord, shown on the right. The tune has a repeat sign with dots on both sides. This tells you to play the first section, then repeat it. When you reach the repeat mark again, ignore it and go on to the second section. Play that twice, too.

First-time and second-time measures

1.	2.
First-time measure sign	**Second-time measure sign**

Some tunes with repeats have two different endings. The first time you play the music, you play the first-time measure, then repeat the section. The second time through, you skip the first-time measure and play the second-time measure instead.

Passamezzo antico

This tune is by Nikolaus Ammerbach (1530-1597), a German composer. It may have been played on an old stringed instrument called a viol, shown here. Check the key signature and look for accidentals. After playing the first-time measure, play from the repeat sign at the beginning. Remember to play the second-time measure when you get to the end.

Dotted eighth notes

A dot after an eighth note makes it half as long again. A dotted eighth note usually has a sixteenth note joined to it, to make up one quarter note beat. Try clapping the dotted rhythm on the right a few times, to get used to it. Fit the sixteenth note in by saying a short "and" just before the next beat.

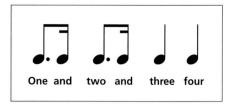

One and two and three four

Practice piece

Practice this short tune to get used to playing the dotted eighth note rhythm. Play each dotted eighth note and sixteenth note in one bow. Be precise when you change fingers and bow direction.

The Trout Quintet

This tune is by the Austrian composer Franz Schubert (1797-1828). It is from a quintet (a piece for five players, each playing a separate line of music). Remember to play the first section of the tune twice. When you get to the repeat sign, save some bow for the next note, which is another up bow. Do this whether you are repeating the music or continuing straight to the second section.

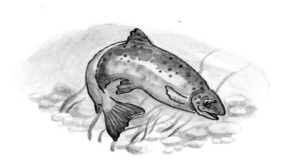

"From the New World"

This tune is from a symphony called *From the New World*, by a Czech composer, Antonin Dvořák (1841-1904). It was first performed at Carnegie Hall, New York, shown here. *Largo* means "slow and stately".

Trumpet tune

This tune is by Henry Purcell. The word *maestoso* means "majestically". Play loudly and confidently, using a separate bow for each note. There are new down bows at the beginning of lines two and three. Look out for the F sharp accidentals, too.

Using your fourth finger

The tunes on these pages have notes which you play with your fourth finger. The notes D, A and E, shown on the right, are open string notes, but you can play them with your fourth finger instead. To do this, you have to put your fourth finger down on the string below the open string note. If your violin is in tune, the fourth finger note and the open string note should both sound the same.

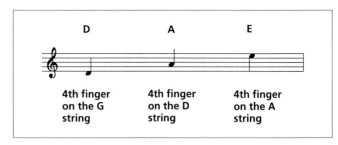

Using your fourth finger can make tunes easier to play. This is because you can play on one string for more of the time, without moving your bow to another string. Sometimes though, the order of the notes makes it easier to play an open string instead.

Make sure there is a space between your third and fourth fingers.

Practice piece

In this short piece, you have to play fourth finger notes and open string notes. Listen carefully to check that you are playing in tune.

Folk song

There are lots of fourth finger notes in this folk tune from Central Europe. Only use your fourth finger when the music tells you to. When you play top E followed by B, keep your first finger down and just move your fourth finger. Practice these notes to get used to the big stretch and the sound.

William Tell

This tune is by the Italian composer Gioacchino Rossini (1792-1868). *William Tell* is an opera (a play in which most of the words are sung). The music has lots of instructions to follow, and there is an end part called a coda. Find out more on the right.

Codas

A coda goes at the end of a piece. Play the next tune with all the repeats. When you get to D.C. *al Coda*, go back to the very beginning and play until you reach "To coda ⊕". Then jump to the last line where it says "⊕ Coda" and play to the end.

Theme from symphony no.11

This tune is by the Austrian composer Joseph Haydn (1732-1809). The sign after the treble clef stands for "common time". It means the same as 4/4 (four quarter notes in a measure). You only need to play a fourth finger E some of the time. There is a new fourth finger note too. Find out more on the right.

New note

The new note in the tune below is another B. Play it using your fourth finger on the E string.

Triplets

The notes on the left with a "3" over them are called triplets. You have to fit three notes into one beat, and the notes must be of equal length.

Staccato bowing

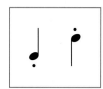

A dot above or below a note tells you to make it short, or "staccato". To do this, stop the bow after each stroke. Don't play staccato notes louder than other notes.

Minuet in G

The German composer Johann Sebastian Bach (1685-1750) wrote this dance tune for his wife. It is from the book of music shown on the right, which was dedicated to her. In the last line, the triplets are slightly faster than the eighth notes. Look for staccato notes.

Skaters' waltz

Ask a friend to play *German Dance*, opposite, while you play *Skaters' Waltz*. *Legato* means "smoothly".

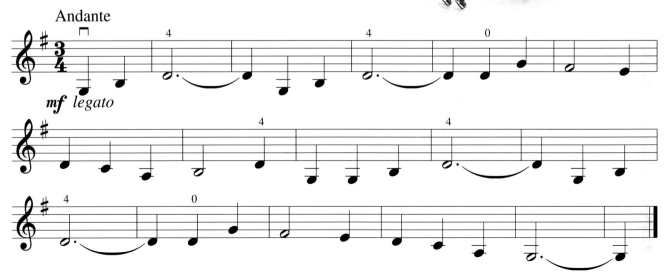

Scheherazade

This tune is by the Russian composer Nikolay Rimsky-Korsakov (1844-1908). It is based on a story called *The Arabian Nights*. There are some long tied notes in this piece, so remember to count carefully and move your bow slowly.

German dance

You could play this tune while a friend plays the tune opposite. See page 37 for more about playing together.

Decorating music

Ornaments are decorations that can be added to music to make it more interesting. You can find out how to play different types of ornaments on the next four pages. Try playing the tunes without the ornaments first, to get used to the rhythms. Once you feel confident, add the ornaments.

Grace notes

The very small notes in the next tune are ornaments called grace notes. You play them very quickly, just before the next beat. Play the grace notes and the main note all in one bow.

Waltz

There are grace notes in this waltz by Brahms. You could ask someone to clap quarter note beats while you play, to help you get the rhythm right.

Trills

The sign 𝒕𝒓 is an ornament called a trill. To play a trill, you play the note on which the trill is written and the note above it. Play one note then the other again and again, as fast as you can, in one long bow. You have to do this for as long as the note with the trill sign lasts, so don't forget to count.

Variation on "La follia"

This tune, based on an old Italian folk song, is by Arcangelo Corelli (1653-1713), shown here. Corelli was one of the first people to make violin playing and violin music popular. This piece has lots of triplets, and a trill at the end. *Adagio* means "slowly".

Winter

This tune is from *The Four Seasons*, a set of four violin pieces by the Italian composer and violinist Antonio Vivaldi (1678-1741). The pieces describe the way the seasons change throughout the year. There is another one on page 34.

Violin makers

The first violins were made in the 16th century. The shape of the violin has only changed very slightly since then.

Three of the most famous violin makers were Italians called Nicolo Amati (1596-1684), Antonio Stradivari (around 1644-1737) and Giuseppe Guarneri (1698-1744). Although other Europeans made fine instruments too, these men made the best violins ever. The record price ever paid at an auction for one of Stradivari's violins is $1,590,800.

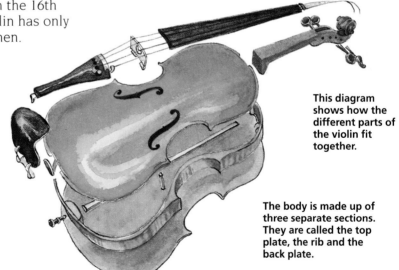

This diagram shows how the different parts of the violin fit together.

The body is made up of three separate sections. They are called the top plate, the rib and the back plate.

Who made yours?

If you look through the sound holes of your violin, you may see a label inside. This tells you the name of the person who made your violin, where they made it and when. Your violin may be a copy of one by a famous violin maker.

> Antonius Stradivarius Cremonenfis
> Faciebat Anno 17 2 4

This label inside one of Antonio Stradivari's violins tells you that he made it in Cremona, Northern Italy, in 1724. The words are in an old language called Latin.

Mordents

The sign on the left is another ornament, called a mordent. It is like a short trill. You play the note on which the mordent is written, then the note above it, then the original note again. Do this quickly, all in one bow. You can see how to play a mordent on the right.

Gavotte

This dance tune is by Purcell. He was the organist at Westminster Abbey, in London, shown on the right. The word *allegretto* at the beginning of the music means "fairly quickly". There are lots of mordents in this piece. Look through it before you start playing, to check where they are. Make sure that you play the staccato notes, too.

Allegretto

Lament

A lament is a sad song. To help make this tune sound sad, play it slowly and use long flowing bows. Look for the tied notes, the accidentals and the trill. The sign **pp** at the end stands for *pianissimo*, which means "very quietly". Try to play as quietly as you can in the last measure.

Adagio

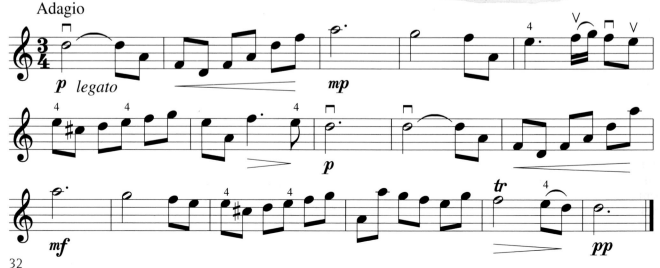

Acciaccaturas

On the left, the very small note with the line through it is an ornament called an acciaccatura ("a-chak-a-too-ra"). The name comes from an Italian word meaning "to crush". Play the acciaccatura as quickly as possible, just before the main note it is joined to. Play both notes with one bow.

Song of the reapers

You have to play acciaccaturas in this tune by the German composer Robert Schumann (1810-1856). Remember to repeat the first line of music.

Allegretto

Playing new tunes

Playing a piece of music which you have never seen before is called sight reading. Before you start to play a new tune, take the time to look through the music carefully first. Watch for clues which tell you how you should play it. Then, when you are ready, play the piece all the way through without stopping, even if you make mistakes. On the right, you can see some of the things to look for.

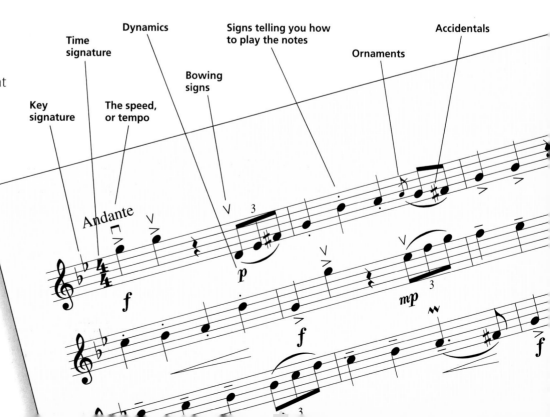

New notes

The new notes on these pages are B flat played on the E string and E flat played on the A string. Find out how to play them on the right.

A new finger pattern

To play the B flat and E flat shown on the left, put your fourth finger down close to your third finger, so that both fingers touch. You have to do this a lot in the next tune. Look at the picture below to make sure that you position your fourth finger correctly.

Use this hand position in the next tune. Pull your first finger back on the A string, to play the lower B flat.

Autumn

There are B flats in this tune from *The Four Seasons* by Vivaldi, but no E flats. There is an optional new note, high C, in the second line, in parentheses. To play it, stretch your fourth finger as far as you can on the E string, but try not to let the other fingers move. If this is too difficult, play the note A below, instead.

Chanson triste

This tune is by Tchaikovsky, shown here. Its title means "Sad song". Watch for the B flats and E flats. In line three, play F with your first finger, then move it up slightly to play F sharp. In the next measure, put your second finger close to your first, to play G.

Gavotte

Look for the accidentals in this dance tune by Bach. There are some tricky notes in the last two measures of the second line and in the last three measures of the tune. Practice these parts on their own.

A new sign

If you see a note in violin music with a short line above or below it, make it sound a little more important than the ones around it. There are many ways to do this. You can bow more firmly to make the note a little louder, or leave a tiny gap between the marked note and the next.

Farandole

This tune is by Bizet, shown on the right. It was written for L'Arlésienne, a play by the French writer Daudet. Remember to emphasize all of the notes which have a short line above or below them.

Jesu, joy of man's desiring

Bach, shown here conducting his church choir, wrote this tune for the organ. It is in 9/8 time, so there are nine eighth note beats in a measure, arranged in three groups of three. Practice the notes slowly first, especially those in the first-time measures. Remember to repeat the tune, playing the second-time measure at the end. There is a part for a second player, opposite.

36

Playing together

Before you play music with someone else, learn your own part carefully. Check that your instruments are in tune with each other. Make sure you both play in time. Listen to each other while you play, so you can hear how the parts fit together. You could switch parts, to help you get to know the music better.

Farandole (Duet part)

A tune for two players is called a duet. This tune can be played with *Farandole* on the left, to make a duet. Play steady, emphasized notes, to help the other player keep in time. Try not to rush, though.

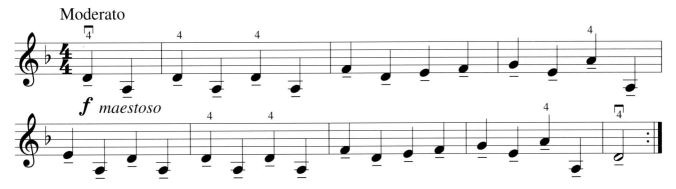

Jesu, joy of man's desiring (Duet part)

This tune can be played with the one opposite, to make a duet. Count the beats carefully all the way through. Make sure you don't rush, as the other player has to fit three eighth notes into each of your dotted quarter notes. Remember to repeat the tune, and don't forget to play the second-time measure when you get to the end.

Bach lived and worked in the town of Leipzig, in Germany, shown here.

Bourrée

This dance tune is from a set of four pieces by Handel, called the *Water Music*. The pieces were first performed on the River Thames, in London, shown on the right. The word *marcato* at the beginning tells you to accent the notes throughout. Remember to do this all the way through the tune, except in the places where the notes are slurred. For the slurred notes, only accent the first note in each pair. There are three different accidentals to look for, too.

Eine kleine Nachtmusik

Mozart composed this piece in 1787. The title is German for "a little night music". On the right, you can see how he wrote down the opening measures of the tune. To help you learn the rhythm, clap it, or play it on one string, while a friend claps steady quarter note beats to keep you in time. When you feel confident, you could ask someone to play the duet part on the opposite page.

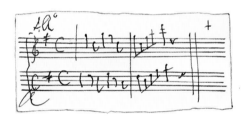

Playing on two strings

Sometimes, you have to play two notes at the same time by bowing two strings at once. The notes are written one above the other in the music. You sometimes have to play an open string and a fingered note together. You can also play a fingered note on each string. Two or more notes played together are called a double stop.

Here, the first finger is on the D string and the second finger is on the A string. The bow plays both strings at once.

Waltz

In this tune, you have to play two notes together. To do this, you count exactly as if you were playing one note. Practice each double stop slowly, moving from one to the other, to get used to the finger patterns.

Eine kleine Nachtmusik (Duet part)

This is the duet part for the tune on the opposite page. Although the rhythm is fairly simple, it is important that you play exactly in time. You must count carefully to fit in the quarter rests, and make sure that you don't rush the eighth notes. Look for the places where you play stops. The picture on the right shows the Augarten concert hall in Vienna, Austria, where Mozart's music was often performed.

39

Changing key signature

Sometimes, the key signature changes part of the way through a piece. When this happens, a new key signature cancels the old one. Concentrate to make sure you play the correct notes.

Humoresque

This tune is by Dvořák, shown here. *Poco lento e grazioso* means "fairly slowly and gracefully". After line six, the key signature changes to B flat and E flat. F sharp becomes F natural. But when you go back to the beginning, play in the original key. *Rit.* (short for *ritardando*) means "slow down", but play at the original speed when you return to the top.

A new kind of repeat

The instruction D.C. *al Fine* at the end of a piece stands for *Da Capo al Fine*. This tells you to go back to the beginning and start again. Stop playing when you reach the *Fine* sign for the second time.

Syncopation

Syncopation is when there is an unexpected accent on a weak beat of the measure. Jazz music has lots of syncopation in it. In the tunes below, the accents come just before the main beat each time. It may take a little work to play this type of rhythm, but the more you practice it, the easier it will become.

Dotted eighth note rests

Dotted eighth note rest

A dot after an eighth note rest increases its length by half. A dotted eighth rest is one and a half eighth note beats long, or three quarters of a quarter note beat long. Look for them below.

Jazzbo Brown

This is a jazz tune. Jazz is a style of music that developed in America at the end of the 19th century. Play fairly slowly. To help you get the feel of the syncopated rhythm, ask someone to clap four beats in a measure while you play. Remember that the accented notes come just before the main beat.

An early jazz band

Down and out

In each line, you have to use your first finger to play B flat, followed by B natural. At the end of the second line, use your second finger to play C natural followed by C sharp. Don't play too quickly.

Dancing to a jazz band

41

New note

The new note on these pages is C sharp played on the G string. It only appears once in each part of *Canon*. Find out more on the right.

C#

A new finger pattern

To play the new C sharp, stretch your third finger a little farther than when you play C natural. You can check that it is in the right place by putting your fourth finger down to play D. If you do this, your third finger and fourth finger should touch.

Canon

This tune is by the German composer Johann Pachelbel (1653-1706). A canon is another name for a round. It is a piece for two or more instruments, where one starts playing after the other. Ask a friend to play the duet part on the other page with you. *Larghetto* means "fairly slowly".

Duets on your own

If you want to play both parts of the duets in this book by yourself, you could record your playing. Choose one of the parts and practice it. When you feel confident, record the tune. Count a measure out loud on the tape before you start, and make sure you count carefully in your head while you play.

Next, rewind the tape, play it back, and play the second part "live" over the top. The counting you recorded will help you know when to start, and to keep time as you play. You could even tape both parts, one after the other, so you can choose which part to play over the top.

Canon (Duet part)

This is the duet part for the tune on the opposite page. Count the beats for the first four measures, then play in the fifth measure. You have exactly the same tune as the other player, but you play it later. On the right, you can see a picture of Vienna, where Pachelbel worked as an organist.

New notes

The new notes on these pages are G sharp played on the D string, and D sharp played on the A string. Place your third finger in the position shown on page 42. As these notes are quite tricky to play, prepare yourself by checking through the tunes to make sure that you know where they appear.

G#   D#

Minuet in A

This tune by the Italian composer Luigi Boccherini (1743-1805) is part of a string quintet. A friend could play the piano part below, to accompany you.

A string quintet is a piece for five stringed instruments.

Caprice no.24

This tune is by the Italian violinist and composer
Nicolò Paganini (1782-1840), shown on the right.
Some of his music was so difficult that he was the
only person who could play it well. A caprice is a
light-hearted piece of music, written to be played in
a carefree style. Other composers have written tunes
based on this one.

At the end of measures four and eight, take the bow
off the string and start the next measure with a new
down bow. In all the other places with two down
bows, stop the bow between the notes, but do not
take it off.

Music help

This list explains the Italian words used in this book. Each Italian word has its pronunciation after it (in **bold** letters). Read these pronunciation letters as if they were English words.

adagio	**a-dah-jee-oh**	slowly
allegretto	**a-luh-gretto**	fairly quickly
allegro	**a-leg-ro**	quickly
andante	**an-dan-tay**	at a walking pace
con sordino	**con saw-dee-no**	with a mute
crescendo (cresc.)	**cruh-shen-doh**	getting louder
D.C. al Coda	**dee cee al coh-dah**	repeat from the beginning to the coda sign
D.C. al Fine	**dee cee al fee-nay**	repeat from the beginning to the Fine sign
diminuendo (dim.)	**dim-in-you-en-doh**	getting quieter
forte (f)	**for-tay**	loudly
fortissimo (ff)	**for-tiss-im-oh**	very loudly
larghetto	**lah-get-oh**	quite slowly
largo	**lah-go**	slow and stately
legato	**leg-ah-toe**	smoothly
leggiero	**led-jee-air-oh**	lightly
maestoso	**my-stoh-so**	majestically
marcato	**mah-cah-toe**	heavily accented
mezzo forte (mf)	**met-so for-tay**	fairly loudly
mezzo piano (mp)	**met-so pee-ah-no**	fairly quietly
moderato	**mod-er-ah-toe**	at a moderate speed, a little faster than andante
pianissimo (pp)	**pee-an-iss-im-oh**	very quietly
piano (p)	**pee-ah-no**	quietly
pizzicato (pizz.)	**pit-see-cah-toe**	pluck the string
poco lento e grazioso	**poh-coh len-toe ay grat-see-oh-so**	fairly slowly and gracefully
ritardando (rit.)	**rit-ar-dan-doh**	getting slower
staccato	**stack-ah-toe**	short, detached

Scales

Scales are chains of notes that go up and down by steps. There are two kinds of steps in a scale: half steps (semitones) and whole steps (tones). Most of the tunes in this book are based on a kind of scale called a major scale. Each scale is named after the note that it starts and ends on.

If you practice the scales below, you will get used to playing with your fingers in different patterns. Start each one with a down bow. There are finger numbers over the notes. The fingers that you put down close together are shown with short lines between them. Check each key signature before you start to play.

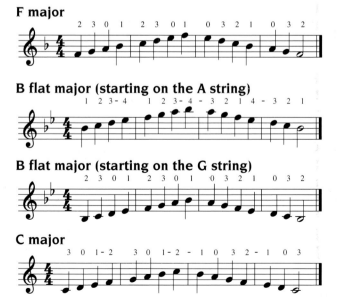

G major

D major

A major

E major

F major

B flat major (starting on the A string)

B flat major (starting on the G string)

C major

Violin music to listen to

Below are some suggestions for violin music to listen to. There is also a list of music for groups of stringed instruments.

Violin music:

Bach	Concerto for two violins
	Partitas for solo violin
	Sonatas for solo violin
Bartók	Duets
Beethoven	Violin Concerto in D
	Romance in F
Brahms	Violin Concerto in D
Bruch	Violin Concertos
Copland	Hoe Down (from *Rodeo*)
Delius	Violin Concerto
Dvořák	Sonatina in G
Grappelli	Any recordings
Kreisler	Praeludium and Allegro
Massenet	Méditation from *Thais* (Act 2)
Mendelsshon	Concerto in E minor
Paganini	Caprice no.24
Sibelius	Violin Concerto
Vivaldi	The Four Seasons
	Any concertos for one, two, three or four violins
Wieniawski	Scherzo Tarantelle

Music for groups of stringed instruments:

Albinoni	Adagio
Bach	Brandenburg Concertos
Barber	Adagio for Strings
Britten	Simple Symphony
Dvořák	Serenade in E
Elgar	Chanson de Matin
	Chanson de Nuit
	Elegy
	Introduction and Allegro
	Serenade in E minor
Grieg	Holberg Suite
Holst	St. Paul's Suite
Mozart	The Hunt Quartet
Schubert	The Trout Quintet
Tchaikovsky	Serenade in C
Tippett	Concerto for Double String Orchestra
Vaughan Williams	Fantasia on a theme by Thomas Tallis
	Fantasia on Greensleeves
Warlock	Capriol Suite

Index of tunes

Aria Allemagna, 23
Autumn, 34
Bell ringing, 7
Bourrée, 38
Cancan, 14
Canon, 42-43
Caprice no.24, 45
Castanet song, 16
Chanson triste, 35
Down and out, 41
Drink to me only, 17
Eine kleine Nachtmusik, 38-39
Farandole, 36-37
Folk song, 26
"From the New World", 25
Gavotte, 32, 35
German dance, 29
Hatikvah, 21
Hither, dear husband, 15
Humming tune, 6
Humoresque, 40
Jazzbo Brown, 41
Jesu, joy of man's desiring, 36-37

Jumping beans, 11
Lament, 32
Le petit rien, 22
Lightly row, 10
Lullaby, 13
March tune, 7
Minuet in A, 44
Minuet in G, 28
Morning has broken, 11
Nocturne, 19
Over the hills and far away, 10
Passamezzo antico, 23
Practice piece, 19, 24, 26
Riding on a donkey, 8
Rigaudon, 7
Russian folk song, 12
Scheherazade, 29
Skaters' waltz, 28
Slumber song, 15
Song of the ass, 16
Song of the reapers, 33
Stepping stones, 13
Strawberry fair, 22
Sumer is icumen in, 20

The conquering hero, 9
The gazelles, 14
The Hunt Quartet, 21
The Londonderry Air, 19
The old brown cow, 9
The Trout Quintet, 24
Theme from symphony no.6, 18
Theme from symphony no.11, 27
Trumpet tune, 25
Two-string waltz, 8
Variation on "La follia", 30
Waltz, 30, 39
What shall we do with the drunken sailor? 17
William Tell, 27
Winter, 31

Index

2/4 time, 12
3/4 time, 6, 8
4/4 time, 6, 27
6/8 time, 17, 20
9/8 time, 36

accents, 21
acciaccatura, 33
accidentals, 22, 33
adagio, 30, 46
allegretto, 32, 46
allegro, 14, 46
Amati, Nicolo, 31
Ammerbach, Nikolaus, 23
andante, 14, 15, 46

Bach, Johann Sebastian,
  28, 35, 36, 37
beats, 6
Beethoven, Ludwig van, 12
Bizet, Georges, 16, 36
Boccherini, Luigi, 44
bourrée, 38
bow, 2, 3, 5
bowing, 6, 12, 13, 18
  arm, 5, 9
  signs, 6, 21, 28, 33, 36
Brahms, Joannes, 13, 30

cancan, 14
canon, 42
caprice, 45
chord, 39
coda, 27
common time, 27
con sordino, 15, 46
Corelli, Arcangelo, 30
Couperin, François, 22
cresc./crescendo, 17

D.C. *al Coda*, 27, 46
D.C. *al Fine* (*Da Capo al
  Fine*), 40, 46
dim./diminuendo, 17
dotted eighth note, 24
  rest, 41
dotted half note, 10
dotted quarter note, 9
  rest, 20

down bow, 6, 18

duet, 37
duets, 28-29, 36-37,
  38-39, 42-43
Dvořák, Antonin, 25, 40
dynamics, 12, 33

eighth note, 8
  dotted, 24
  rest, 15
emphasizing notes, 21, 28, 36

f, 12, 46
ff, 19, 46
finger, numbers, 6
  patterns, 6, 16, 18,
    26, 34, 39, 42
first-time measure, 23
flats, 18, 22
forte, 12, 46
fortissimo, 19, 46
fourth finger notes 26, 27, 34

gavotte, 32, 35
Gay, John, 15
getting louder, 17
getting quieter, 17
grace notes, 30
Guarneri, Giuseppe, 31

half note, 6
  dotted, 10
  rest, 10
Handel, George Frideric, 9, 38
Haydn, Joseph, 27
holding the violin and bow, 5

jazz, 41

key signature, 11, 33
  changing, 40

lament, 32
larghetto, 42, 46
largo, 25, 46
legato, 28, 46
listening to music, 47

maestoso, 25, 46
marcato, 38, 46
measures, 6
Mendelssohn, Felix, 19

mezzo forte, 13, 46
mezzo piano, 22, 46
mf, 13, 46
minuet, 28, 44
moderato, 15, 46
mordent, 32
Mozart, Wolfgang Amadeus,
  21, 38, 39
mp, 22, 46
mute, 15

naturals, 16, 22
note(s), 6
  emphasized, 21, 28, 36
  fourth finger, 26, 27, 34
  length, 6
  open string, 6, 8, 12,
    26, 39
  slurred, 12
  tied, 11

Offenbach, Jacques, 14
open string notes 6, 8,
  12, 26, 39
opera, 27
oratorio, 9
ornaments, 30, 31, 32, 33

p, 13, 46
Pachelbel, Johann, 42, 43
Paganini, Nicolò, 45
pianissimo, 32, 46
piano, 13, 46
pizz./pizzicato, 14, 46
playing,
  loudly, 12
  on two strings, 39
  position, 5
  quietly, 13
  together, 37
poco lento e grazioso, 40, 46
Poglietti, Alessandro, 23
pp, 32, 46
Purcell, Henry, 7, 25, 32

quarter note, 6
  dotted, 9
  rest, 10
quartet, 21
quintet, 24
  string, 44

repeats, 16, 23, 27, 40
rests, 10, 15, 20, 41
rigaudon, 7
Rimsky-Korsakov, Nikolay, 29
rit./ritardando, 40, 46
rosin, 3
Rossini, Gioacchino, 27
round, 20, 42

scales, 46
Schubert, Franz, 24
Schumann, Robert, 33
sea chantey, 17
second-time measure, 23
sharps, 6, 7, 11, 22
shoulder pad, 3
  rest, 3
sight reading, 33
sixteenth note, 22
slurred notes, 12
staccato, 28, 46
stand, how to, 5
Stradivari, Antonio, 31
string quintet, 44
symphony, 18
syncopation, 41

Tchaikovsky, Pyotr
  Il'yich, 18, 35
tempo, 33
tied notes, 11, 12
time signature, 6, 33
trill, 30
triplets, 28
tuning the violin, 4

up-beats, 13
up bow, 6, 18

viol, 23
violin, 2, 3
  extras for, 3
  how to hold, 5
  looking after, 3
  makers, 31
  parts of, 2, 3
  tuning, 4
Vivaldi, Antonio, 31, 34

waltz, 8, 30, 39
whole note, 6

Acknowledgements

The publishers would like to thank Ella Louise Allert,
Gershom Clarke, Samantha Jones and Candy Turner
who were photographed for this book; also
Bridgewood and Neitzert, London, for supplying the
violins in the photographs.

First published in 1995 by Usborne Publishing Ltd, Usborne
House, 83-85 Saffron Hill, London EC1N 8RT, England.
Copyright © 1995 Usborne Publishing Ltd.